Tim Lapp's personal account of his family provides us with a narrow glimpse into how that culture dealt with a disease to which even the Amish are not immune --- alcoholism. I applaud Tim for taking the time and making the effort to document how his father, Manny Lapp, turned the tragedy of his alcoholic father being shunned by the church to a story of triumph over hardship, ridicule, and embarrassment. *Shunning to Shining* is a well-written story of adversity to which many people will be able to relate.

Dr. John M. Anderson,
President, Millersville University

Shunning to Shining brings you to the heart of Lancaster County and into the Amish culture to tell the powerful story that your past doesn't have to determine your future. From the darkness of alcoholism and shunning to the inspiration of a hard-working Amish electrician, the people in this book are authentic, engaging, and inspiring. I thoroughly enjoyed reading Tim's stories, and I believe you will too.

Peter Greer, President & CEO
HOPE International

From life lessons to business lessons, *Shunning to Shining* offers fascinating insights and thoughtful perspectives that left me thinking far past the last page of the book. Tim Lapp has effectively captured the amazing and inspiring journey of his family coupled with the lessons learned along the way. The book is one of hope and optimism around work, family, and the power of a positive attitude.

Tom Baldrige, President & CEO
The Lancaster Chamber of Commerce & Industry

Shunning

to

Shining

An Amish Family's Dark Journey Into Light

Tim Lapp

with Shawn Smucker

Co-written by Shawn Smucker
Edited by Andi Cumbo-Floyd
Cover Design by Peter Pentz
Cover Formatted by Bryan Allain

This book is dedicated in memory of
Uncle Wilmer Lapp,
forever loved and remembered,
for making us all smile and laugh
&
Matt Steller,
true and forever best friend,
who stuck closer than a brother.

TABLE OF CONTENTS

PREFACE

I am an ordinary guy, who has lived an extraordinary and blessed life. Growing up in beautiful Lancaster County was an incredible experience, and I never went through any major hardships during my early years. My parents had a strong marriage, and even though my older brother would take on my twin brother and I in a fight from time to time, I always knew that the five of us were united in love and support.

Life was good.

I didn't experience the loss of a loved one that affected me in a life changing way for the first 40 years of my life. But in January of 2010, that changed. In the span of 12 days, I lost two of the most influential men in my life: first my Pop-Pop Lapp (Christ Lapp, Jr.) and then my dad (Manny Lapp).

Both men shaped me into the man I am today. I am forever grateful to my Heavenly Father for the gift that both of them were to me. You can't choose your family, and I thank God every day for placing me in this Lapp Family.

I decided to write this book about the two most influential

men in my life, but please understand that standing beside these two great men were two equally incredible women. My mom-mom (Rachel Lapp) and my mom (Flossie Lapp) were exceptional women, and I believe that without their selfless love and support their husbands would not have been the men they were. Trust me. I could write a book about them as well.

In the community, everyone knew Christ Lapp, Jr. and Manny Lapp, although for very different reasons. Christ had one reputation, and Manny had another. This is the story about how one became shunned while the other shined bright.

But even my pop-pop found redemption at the end. During the last two years of his life, Pop-Pop and I would often go to the Bird-In-Hand farmer's market to get cup cheese, and he occasionally shared his regrets with me.

One year before he died, I joined Pop-Pop at his assisted living home for communion. I'll never forget that moment, watching him take communion and being so thankful that no matter how far we go, there is always a way back, a way home.

This is the true story of a family that overcame, the story of a family that, only fifty years ago, was looked down on by the community they lived in. The patriarch, my pop-pop, was known as the town drunk, had lost a farm, and even spent time in prison because of his drinking.

But this is also a story of redemption, a story of how my father forged a different life for himself.

This is the true story of my family.

A Family Book
By Elam Stoltzfoos

A family is like a book,
The children are the leaves.
The parents are the covers,
That protection beauty gives.

At first the pages of this book,
Are black and pure and fair.
But times soon writeth memories,
And painteth pictures there.

Love is the little golden clasp,
That bindeth up the trust.
Oh break it not lest all the leaves,
Should scatter and be lost.

PART ONE

SHUNNING

Chapter One

The Story My Father Told Me

My dad, Manny Lapp, told me a story one time, a story I'll never forget.

One night, he had to go to a bar to retrieve his father, my pop-pop. Apparently this was not an uncommon occurrence. On the way home, Pop-Pop became belligerent, protesting in slurred words that he didn't want to go home yet, that he didn't want anyone to see him that way. He started grabbing for the steering wheel, and the car swerved back and forth.

My father, only a teenager and not even old enough to legally drive, struggled to maintain control of the vehicle. My grandfather became even more animated, so my dad did the only thing he could think to do: he hauled off and punched his own dad. Knocked him out. Pop-Pop slumped over against the door and didn't move until they got home.

"My father is the only man I ever punched in the face," my dad told me, and those words brought tears to his eyes. He wasn't proud of the fact, but it was part of our family history, and I guess he felt it was important for me to hear about it.

I have to wonder what went through my dad's mind as he drove the rest of the way home, his father silent in the seat beside him, unconscious. I have to wonder what that felt like for my dad.

The story of my dad punching his own father planted a seed in me, a desire to find out more about my family. I realized in that moment that I didn't know as much about my father or my family as I might have thought. I wondered what other stories were buried in the not-so-distant past.

I wanted to know more.

Before I wrote this book, I didn't know to what extent my pop-pop was affected by his alcoholism. For example, I had never heard the stories about him going to prison. But when I started to dig a little bit, when I started stirring around, a lot of things about my family drifted to the surface.

When it comes to telling these stories about our family, I feel a little bit like how my dad probably felt telling me the story about how he punched his own father. Some of these stories, they're not happy stories. They're not things that will make you feel good. They're things that maybe some families might be embarrassed about or try to hide or at least never talk about – a drunken grandfather who spent time in prison and lost the farm; a family that was kicked out of the Amish; kids whose schoolmates made fun of them because of who their father was. You know, at one point when my dad was trying to start Lapp Electric, three different banks told him they wouldn't loan him money because his father was Christ Lapp.

The town drunk.

The man who couldn't keep it together.

Those aren't fun things to live through, and they're not fun to talk about. But if you don't know where you've come from, it can be tough to get a handle on where you're going. If you don't know your history, be careful! It might come back to haunt you.

Of course, it's not all doom and gloom. There are some really wonderful things about my family, many things that make me smile, make me proud to be who I am. There are stories that make me laugh, stories of overcoming and working hard and beating the odds.

I want to tell these stories (all of them – the good as well as the bad) because they're the stories that made my father into the man he became. They are the stories that in some ways defined our Lapp family for many years, and they're the stories that motivated my father, along with his brothers and sisters, to live a better life, to work harder, to break free from those things that tried to hold them back. They didn't let their past define who they could become. In fact, all my dad's siblings were extremely strong. They were a close-knit group of brothers and sisters. Four of them even started and owned their own restaurants in Lancaster County. The "sins of the father" would not keep them down.

You can overcome your past, too. It doesn't have to limit you. It can propel you. No matter what you've been through, it doesn't have to hold you back—it can motivate you to become better, to move forward.

That's what it did for my dad Manny Lapp. Somewhere along the way, he became a great husband, a wonderful father, and maybe even the first Amish electrician.

He went from shunning to shining.

If he could do it, anyone can.

Chapter Two

I'm Going Home

In Pop-Pop's last days, when he was nearing the end of his life, I went to visit him. He was doing physical therapy across the street from the Lancaster General health campus. He was there for three or four weeks that December because he needed some extra rehab away from where he lived at Evergreen Estates in Bridgeport. He was 91 years old.

He was in physical therapy for a recent operation. He also suffered from emphysema, something he had gotten from the non-filtered Camels he smoked for so many years. I think he started smoking when he was 14. I used to smoke cigarettes back in the day, too, and sometimes he'd bum a smoke off me. I'd hand him one of my Marlboro Lights, and he'd rip the filter off before smoking it.

"That's not good for you, Pop-Pop," I said, but he just shook his head, inhaling deeply and then exhaling with relief, the smoke swirling around his face. That's one thing about Pop-Pop – he did things his own way, the way he wanted to do them. I don't know if I ever saw him change his mind or his approach based on something anyone told him.

But that was years before. I had stopped in to see Pop-Pop while he was in physical therapy during the first week of January in 2010 because my aunts had been talking about how unhappy he was there. I thought maybe I'd head in there and try to cheer him up a little.

Let me tell you this: Pop-Pop was brutally honest in his criticism of other people. Whether it be their weight, how they talked, or how they looked, he'd just say whatever came to his mind. It could be pretty embarrassing sometimes.

"How's it going, Pop-Pop?" I asked him when I went into the room where the nurses were putting him through his paces. They stood beside him, encouraging him and trying to help him walk. He glared at everyone, me included.

"They treat you like animals in here," he said in a loud voice. The nurses were right there beside him, and I cringed.

"Easy, Pop-Pop," I said, but the nurses weren't fazed.

Pop-Pop finally did what they asked him to do, but he was just going through the motions. All they wanted him to do was walk five steps, but he wouldn't do it without making a big fuss.

"This isn't right," he kept complaining, which was kind of ironic because if I ever complained he said, "Tell your troubles to Jesus."

"Pop-Pop, just do it," I said. "It's for your own good."

He got through the half-hour session and was angry about the whole thing. Right before I left, I hugged him as I did whenever I said good-bye to him in those last years.

"I love you, Pop-Pop," I said. Usually he said "I love you" back to me, but that time he didn't. I think he was still upset about the physical therapy. So I said good-bye and left.

About a week later, I got a call. I looked at my phone and based on the caller ID I thought it was my Aunt Feenie.

"Hello?" I said, expecting to hear my aunt's happy voice.

But it wasn't my aunt. It was Pop-Pop, calling from her phone.

"Tim," he said with excitement in his voice. "I'm going home!"

"Good news, Pop-Pop," I said. "That's awesome."

I could tell he was excited to be going back to Evergreen Estates. But the way he said it, well, I'd remember those words in a few weeks' time.

"I'm going home," he said again, and there was a joy I hadn't heard in his voice for a long time. Maybe never before. We didn't talk long that day. I guess he just wanted to share the news with me.

Two days later, they found him. He had collapsed in his shower, early in the morning. He was gone.

He had been right. He was going home.

Chapter Three
The Boy Who Never Grew Up

My pop-pop was born in 1918 and was promptly named after his father: Christian Lapp, Jr. He was called Christ by his friends, Pop by his kids and most of the grandkids, and Pop-Pop by my brothers and I.

I was born in 1970; there were a lot of years between those two birthdays, a lot of years between the birth of my grandfather and the birth of me. By the time I got to know him, Pop-Pop was in his late fifties and worked in a machine shop across the street from where I lived.

As a child, I knew nothing of his drunken behavior or the fact that he had gotten kicked out of the Amish church. To me, he was the old man I loved, the man who came over to our house on his lunch break with a few sandwiches. He shared them with me, and they tasted kind of like burnt metal from the shop, but it wasn't a bad taste – it was just Pop-Pop.

I remember that vividly.

The Pop-Pop that I knew and loved was a far different man than the one his own children had grown up with.

He was born into the Amish community during the last year of World War I. It wasn't a great time to be Amish. Their stand as pacifists and their determination not to fight in the war had many people treating them like outcasts. Some Amish men were even thrown into prison when they wouldn't enlist.

But you know, in those early days of the 20th century, nothing was easy, not for anyone – it didn't matter if you were Amish or not. For example, in the early 1900s, for every 1,000 births, 100 children died before they reached their first birthday.

Those were hard years.

My pop-pop was born during a time when you often lost many of the people you loved. He was born into a family that had already lost three children: Barbara was born in 1908 and died in 1915 at the age of seven, Rachel was born in 1914 and died one year later; and Jonas, born in 1916, died in 1917.

I wonder about that family, and I wonder what it must have been like to have your own children dying like that, every few years or so. I can't imagine the pain or heartache my great-grandparents must have experienced. I can't help but wonder what kind of a home my grandfather was born into when the home had already experienced so much death.

Were his parents numb to the pain by 1918, or were the wounds still fresh? Did they hold Christ and see the children who had passed?

My pop-pop arrived into the world with only one older living sibling, a brother named Joshua who was nine when pop-pop was born. But only four years later, Joshua was killed by a car. The folks who remember these things say he was the first Amish person in Lancaster County to be killed by an automobile. Those were strange days indeed, with the first cars driving along the roads, soon to be followed by the first airplanes soaring in the blue skies above the fields.

Christ Lapp Sr., my great-grandfather, had gone to market regularly in those days, but after his son Joshua was killed by the automobile, he stopped going. No one knows why. He decided he wanted to stay home, and that was that. Maybe he'd reached his breaking point. Maybe he wanted to stay at home to watch over his son Christ. Maybe he had decided he needed to keep a close eye on his only living son when he had already lost four children. Who knows?

My pop-pop would lose one other sister during his childhood: Lydia, in 1924, when he was six. All in all, only three of those eight Lapp children survived their childhood: my grandfather, his sister Mary, and his younger brother John.

Three out of eight.

Pop-Pop would go on to have eight children of his own.

My dad was one of those eight. What if only three of them had survived? Which aunts and uncles would I have known and loved, and which would have passed before I was born? Or would my dad have been one of the children to die young, snuffing out my own existence?

Three out of eight.

I first learned about this while sitting across the table from my father's cousin Lydia Esh, daughter of my grandfather's younger brother John. I was searching for stories, searching for answers, meeting with aunts and uncles, a great-uncle, a few of my father's cousins. It was one of the most powerful things I have ever done, searching for those stories. I thought I knew what I would find, for the most part, but this realization that my Pop-Pop had lost so many siblings was a revelation to me.

I felt like I had a completely new perspective on who my grandfather was and what his childhood may have been like. I had always heard stories about him, tales blurred by the years of his bad reputation, but as I dug deeper into his life I couldn't help but wonder if the tragedy that surrounded his entrance into the world hadn't played a large part in who he had become.

The farm where Pop-Pop grew up, along Horseshoe Road, was bought long before his birth by a man named Solomon Stoltzfus in 1850 or 1851. Old Solomon had one child, a daughter Barbara, so when Christian Miller of Stumptown said he wanted to marry Barbara, Solomon told him that was okay, but he'd have to move on to the farm and take it over. The young suitor agreed, and as the years passed, he and Barbara had two daughters, and the farm passed to their son-in-law, my great-grandfather, Christian Lapp Sr.

My pop-pop was raised right there, on that farm, with his brother John and his sister Mary and the memory of five siblings who were no more. Later, after many years passed and my great-aunt Mary took over the farm, she was so well-off that people referred to that farm as the "Bank of Horseshoe Road."

There's a story about someone mentioning Pop-Pop in connection with that farm.

"That's the farm where Christ Lapp grew up," one man said.

"Well, that's not true," another man said. "I don't know that Christ Lapp ever grew up."

That seemed to be a pretty common belief among the Amish my grandfather's age. He just never grew up. He couldn't quite lay down the things of his adolescence, and when those things like alcoholism carried over into his adulthood, everything was tainted by them. It was something he admitted as he got older.

"When I was a boy," Pop-Pop once whispered to his niece's husband in a confidential tone of voice, "you didn't know me, but I was a little mischievous."

That may be the understatement of his entire life.

Chapter Four

The Amish Poet-Preacher

While my grandfather grew up (or not, as some might say) on that farm, not too far away there was an Amish preacher named Elam Stoltzfoos and his wife. They had four children: Levi, Rachel, Moses, and Wilmer.

That preacher Elam, he preached like no other Amish preacher of his time, and he wrote poems that would eventually be collected and bound into a small book called *Golden Sunset*, not because Elam wanted to have a book made, but because so many people were asking him for copies of his poems and he didn't have time to copy them all by hand.

The small booklet was printed in 1980 by Pequea Publishers in Gordonville, PA, and this is the Foreward:

FOREWARD

The edit-author, a widely known minister, has exercised a talent of devoted hymnology. During his forty-three years experience of fluent Scripture expound he gained the creativeness of blending suitable hymns to Scripture early. Perhaps it was in that course and during his many travels that he collected more to his treasury, on a bit by bit basis.

It is not known when his first poem book emerged but with years it grew to a 140-page, standard-size notebook, well written in fine penmanship.

In recent years younger ministers requested copies of these collections. The demand for these gems grew beyond ready supply. It is said that he wrote over 60 notebooks, mostly for young ministers. Recently, young ministers have asked permission to bring them to print. With glowing humility he answered that it should not be in his lifetime. Becoming overwhelmed with requests he finally, early this year, gave permission.

The German hymns are gathered from a wider field than ordinarily used hymnbook texts of our church. Many are taken from other German Reformed versions.

Some hymns are re-edited, some reauthored and some completely authorized by Stoltzfoos.

May his evening years be transformed to a Golden Sunset by these Glowing Gems.

The author of the book, Elam Stoltzfoos, was my great-grandfather, my grandmother's father. I haven't heard of many Amish people who have written their own books, and even fewer poem-writing Amish preachers, but I'm proud to have one in my family tree. Reading his words, I feel like I've gotten to know him a little bit.

Here are a few of the poems and hymns published in *Golden Sunset*:

Why I Write

By Elam Stoltzfoos

When folks ask me why I write,

And suggest it's a waste of time.

I say it makes me happy,

To compare each little rhyme.

Then I try to tell them,

That it means a lot to me.

To put down on paper,

All the beauties that I see.

For a flaming far off sunset,

Only lingers for an hour.

And who can keep from fading,

The beauty of a flower?

While the poet all alone,

With his feeble little pen.
Can make the sunset linger,
So if someone gets some pleasure,
From the poem that I have penned.
Then I am doing all these writings
For the purpose I intend.

My Choice
By Elam Stoltzfoos

I want my breakfast served at eight,
With ham and eggs upon the plate.
A well-filled steak I'll eat at once,
And dine again when the day is done.

I want an ultra modern home,
And in each room a telephone.
And then I'll get a small T.V.
Of course I'm careful what I see.

A crazy patch of lovely things,
Like easy chairs with inner springs,
Soft carpets too upon the floor,
And pretty drapes upon the floor.

I want my wardrobe too to be,
Of finest neatest quality.
With latest style in suit and vest,
Why shouldn't Christians have the best?

But then the Master I can see,
In no uncertain voice so clear.
I bid you come and follow me,
The lonely man of Galilee.

Birds of the air have made their nests,
And foxes in the holes find rest.
But I can offer you no bed.
No place for you to lay your head.

In shame I hung my head and cried,
How could I spurn the crucified?
Could I forget the way He went,
The sleepless nights in prayer He spent?

Forty days without a bite,
Alone He fasted day and night.
And did not stop until veil He rent,
Despised, rejected, but on He went.

A man of sorrows and of grief

No earthly friend to bring relief.
Smitten of God the Prophet said,
Mocked, beaten, bruised, His blood ran red.

If He be God and died for me,
No sacrifice too great for me.
For me a mortal man to make,
I'd do it all for Jesus' sake.

Yes, I will tread the path He trod,
No other place will please my God.
So henceforth this my choice will be,
My choice for all Eternity.

A Year's End

By Elam Stoltzfoos

The old ends a new begins,
With pages clear and white.
And what is written on each page,
Will now depend on you.

You can't relive the year that's past,
Erasing every wrong
For once a year or day is past,

It is forever gone.

But don't give up in despair,
If you have failed some test.
Seek God's forgiveness and resolve
Henceforth to do your best.

Resolve each precious day to do
Things good and kind and true
Though days and years may pass away,
These things shall still endure.

You know not where your path may lead
Nor what's beyond the hill
But know that God walks to your side,
If you but do His will.

All things are possible with God,
Though days be bright and dim
So do your part and know that you,
Can leave the rest to Him.

My grandmother Rachel, Elam Stoltzfoos's daughter, had a little brother Wilmer, and he was much younger than the other children. But he still remembers when my pop-pop started paying visits to his sister. Wilmer would stretch up and look out the window, and there came Christ down the driveway in his horse and buggy. Wilmer was only six years old.

They were a popular Amish couple, Christ and Rachel. He was outgoing, and she was deeply loved by her friends. But there was a gray cloud surrounding the proceedings. Apparently, Pop-Pop already had a bit of a reputation for being a black sheep, even that early in his life. I think his father-in-law, Elam Stoltzfoos, was concerned. After all, Elam was a preacher at the Amish church where his son-in-law and daughter would join if they were married.

Still, they were married, and Rachel's younger brother Wilmer remembers the wedding day. "I was a bit excited, and I wondered what for man this man was going to be to take my sister away from the house. Christ didn't have the best reputation, and my father didn't approve of the way he lived."

Even in his disapproval, it doesn't seem that my great-grandfather Elam Stoltzfoos made any particular moves to keep the two apart. That said, I guess we'll never know the private conversations that took place between father and daughter in the days leading up to the wedding. And once they were married, it seems as though Elam Stoltzfoos did everything he could to try and help the situation.

For example, once Christ and Rachel were married, they moved onto Rachel's father's farm, and that would have been their own farm for the foreseeable future if Pop-Pop had been able to keep his life together. That farm was theirs, if they could have stayed Amish, if my grandfather could have gotten his drinking under control. And if they could have stayed Amish, who knows, maybe my father never would have been an electrician. Maybe even I would be Amish.

I recently heard a story from those days, a story about how an Amish man went into a school board meeting held by Conestoga Valley School District. The Amish man was my pop-pop.

"I heard you are looking for land to expand the school grounds," Pop said to the school board. "I'd be willing to sell you my farm, if you're interested."

He was actually talking about his father-in-law's farm, the farm that would be his as long as he stayed Amish. The school board said they would take his offer into consideration.

The next week there was a different Amish man at the school board meeting.

"I'm Christ Lapp's father-in-law," he said. "And I heard my son-in-law was here at the last meeting offering to sell the farm. Well, you should know that he doesn't own that farm; he just lives there. I own the farm, and I told him that I'd give him that farm if he quit his drinking, but he hasn't quit yet, so you'll need to deal with me."

It's hard to say exactly when the bottle began getting the

best of Pop-Pop. But one thing is true: he and Rachel had a hard road ahead.

Pop-Pop married Rachel on November 30th, 1939, and not long after that, his brother John fell during a barn raising. John was only 15 years old, and while he didn't lose his life, this injury caused long-term damage to his mind. He started having seizures, and the seizures grew worse and worse as the years passed.

When John was 19, he got married. But his mental state declined, and the seizures became too much for them to deal with at home, so John went to the Harrisburg State Hospital, which was known as Pennsylvania State Lunatic Hospital from 1851 - 1937. By then, he already had children, and his daughter Lydia remembers him coming home once to visit. While he was home, he had a violent fit of epilepsy, and he was handcuffed and led away. I guess that's how they dealt with those things in those days. That was the last time she saw him outside of the hospital.

The Harrisburg State Hospital was the first public facility in PA to house those deemed mentally ill. It was a massive, three-story brick building with huge white pillars rising up the front. At its largest, the hospital was surrounded by 1,000 acres and was made up of over 70 buildings. By the time my great-uncle John arrived, the hospital was well-known for being woefully understaffed. During war time it was 50%

understaffed, and at its very worst, there was one nurse for every 166 patients. At one point, less than one-third of the authorized male staff positions were filled.

The hospital was closed in 2006.

But in the days when institutionalization was much more common than it is today, and before there were medications available for common mental and emotional ailments, Pop-Pop's brother John spent 18 years in the Harrisburg State Hospital. For a while, the hospital operated its own self-sufficient farm, using the labor of the patients who could work it. It was one of John's favorite things, working that farm, and one of the things he said he missed the most when the farm was shut down.

His wife, my pop-pop's sister-in-law, traveled to see him every single week, either taking the train out of Lancaster or traveling there with another local family who also had a relative in the hospital. By that point, John and his wife owned the farm my pop-pop had grown up on, and even though John was hospitalized, his wife was able to keep the farm operating with the help of her neighbors.

While in the hospital, John didn't want to wear the state clothes provided for him – he preferred dressing in his Amish garb – so his wife took a week's worth of clean clothes to him every time she visited and brought his dirty clothes home to wash. And their life went on from one week to the next like that for many long years.

What kind of an experience must that have been for their family? And beyond that, how did it affect my pop-pop's state of mind? John was his only living brother, and he was locked up in a mental hospital with very little hope of ever being released.

John's daughter Lydia doesn't remember any specific instances of her father being treated poorly in the hospital. In fact, she thought he was treated rather well. But my pop-pop didn't see it that way.

"He was treated like an animal in that place," Pop-Pop would proclaim for the rest of his life whenever he spoke about his brother. "An animal, I tell you."

To be fair, he made the same claim against the nurses who provided him with physical therapy just before he passed away. I was sitting there with him, and he didn't do much to disguise his disgust. He never did.

"They treat you like animals in here," he practically shouted. "It's animal cruelty."

"Pop-Pop, that's not true," I said.

"The nurses are a pain, too."

"Easy, Pop-Pop," I said. "The nurses are right there."

But that didn't stop him.

"Animals, I tell you!"

Pop-Pop's brother John was held in a room there at the hospital, and that's where he died. Of Pop-Pop's seven siblings, only his unmarried sister Mary remained.

Chapter Five

God With Us

Pop-Pop used to always say, "One boy is a boy. Two boys are half a boy. Three boys are none." I had two brothers, and Pop-Pop said this because sometimes he'd ask my dad to send over one of us boys to help him rake leaves or do some work around the house. My dad would say, "Okay, I'll send all three of them over."

"No, no, no," Pop-Pop insisted. "Just give me one boy. One boy's a boy. You get two boys working, and you actually only get half a day's work because they'll be fighting or playing with each other. If you send all three over, I might as well just go out and do it myself. Three boys together can't get any work done."

My pop-pop knew something about raising boys, I guess. He had four of them himself, along with four daughters. They raised quite the family there on the farm owned by his father-in-law the preacher.

"I remember Dad kicked us out of bed early to go milk the cows," Pop-Pop's oldest son Elam said. "There were fifteen to twenty cows, and he pushed us out the door around five in the morning. Just about the time we wrapped up the milking, Mom had breakfast ready for us, so we'd go in and eat."

"What did you have for breakfast?" I asked my uncle Elam.

"Oh, coffee soup," he said with a grin.

"Coffee soup?"

"Yeah, you took crumbled up bread and rolled it into a ball, then put it in a bowl and poured coffee on it with a little milk and sugar. That was breakfast."

Coffee soup.

"After breakfast, I had to go back out and plow the fields. At twelve years old, I was plowing the fields with four horses – whenever I hit a rock, it just about shot me up off the plow."

In 1943, in the midst of Pop-Pop's drinking and troubles with the Amish, when Naomi and Elam were the only children and still small, my father was born right there in the farmhouse where the family lived. My grandmother Rachel held my father on her lap and Pop-Pop was there, too, in those first moments of my dad's life. Naomi came into the room to see the new baby.

"What are we going to name him?" Naomi asked her mother.

"Emanuel," Rachel said with a faraway look in her eye. "Emanuel. It means 'God with us'."

Naomi was there when my father was born, and I think he had a special place in her heart after that.

"Manny never did anything wrong," Naomi recently told me with a grin. "But Elam? Well, he was trouble. He shot me in the butt with a BB gun."

"Just one time!" Elam protested.

"Just one time?" Naomi asked in a doubtful voice. "Maybe. But Manny never did anything like that."

Being Amish never stopped Pop-Pop from mingling with non-Amish folks. For many years, he had a potato business, owned a truck, and employed a driver to take him on deliveries. He'd load up potatoes from their garden and take them into big cities where he had existing customers, places like Baltimore or Philadelphia. On Friday and Saturday, he'd take the horse and buggy into downtown Lancaster to sell butchered chickens and whatever potatoes he hadn't offloaded in the bigger cities.

Pop-Pop had regular customers in town, folks who bought chicken from him every week. This city business was also one of the main reasons they had the ducks. One year, he had fifty customers waiting for their Thanksgiving duck. He was a business man, and who knows how successful he would have been if he hadn't had that problem with alcohol.

One day, he pulled up outside of a bar and went in, leaving young Elam in the back of the buggy. The horse took off, probably spooked by traffic. It ran and ran down the city streets, the buggy bouncing along behind it, Elam holding on for dear life. Eventually, the horse stopped on its own, and Pop-Pop retrieved it, and they headed for home.

The family grew, and they stayed there on the farm. Child after child arrived, and everyone had to work just a little harder. Naomi still remembers the day their youngest sibling arrived. She ran into the room just after he was born, then sprinted outside and screamed to where her brothers and sisters were working outside:

"We have a baby brother!"

Everyone was so excited, and they came running to meet the newest addition. They named him Christian after his father and grandfather, but he'd always go by Christy.

The four boys (Elam, Manny, Wilmer, and Christy) shared a room, and the four girls (Naomi, Feenie, Anna Mary, and Barbie) shared a room. None of the rooms had closets, and there wasn't a bathroom upstairs. There was no central heat – you snuggled up under the covers the best you could, and in the winter it got cold, which actually wasn't too bad, at least not until you had to get out of bed to get dressed in the morning. Then the kids would race downstairs and crowd around the coal stove, the only heat in the house. They stood there as long as they could, trying to warm up, their breath fogging up around them.

Even with their father's drinking problem, their childhood was anything but sad. They seemed to compensate for their father by taking care of each other. Feenie remembers playing Rook almost every night and running around outside as a little kid. A lady named Mrs. Warren used to come every Christmas, her trunk full of gifts. On Christmas morning they raced downstairs, and every year they found a plate waiting for each child on the long bench, and each plate held an orange and a candy cane.

Manny's brother Wilmer had ponies on the farm, and their neighbor Ray Atkins brought his old Willys Jeep down and let Christy drive it through the fields. Every night the kids all walked up to Ray's house and watched *Bonanza*.

Chapter Six

When Pop-Pop Left

They worked hard in those days, my dad and his brothers and sisters. My aunts were in charge of the chickens and gathering the eggs. If there was going to be chicken that night for dinner, my dad's sister Naomi was often the one to go outside, pick out a bird, and chop off its head.

Every spring, they got 50 ducks and Naomi took care of them. One morning, Naomi went out to the small house the ducks were kept in and found all of them dead. A weasel had snuck in somehow and killed every single duck. She just stood there staring for the longest time, then went and told Pop-Pop.

He absolutely lost it.

"You should have closed the door!" he shouted.

"I did close the door," she protested. But he refused to listen, and Naomi cried all day about those ducks. She was

31

only ten or eleven years old, but Pop-Pop wasn't one to show much mercy.

It was about that time when Naomi realized Pop-Pop had a drinking problem. She woke up at 3am and realized a light was on downstairs. She thought that seemed odd, so she crept to the lower level and peeked into the kitchen. Her mother Rachel was sitting on a wooden bench behind the stove, crying.

"What's wrong?" Naomi asked, walking over, sitting beside her.

"Your dad left," Rachel said, gathering her composure. "He came home drunk and then left with someone else to go drink some more."

There would be many more such evenings, many late-night returns, many loud sounds as Pop-Pop rummaged through the house looking for some money so that he could pay the taxi driver who had brought him home. One night the cab fare was $300. Another time he got on the train and was gone all weekend. Rachel didn't know where he was or what he was doing.

Elam, the second oldest (and oldest son), was hit particularly hard by his father's drinking. When he was only 13 years old, he and his father went to a hunting cabin in Lewistown, 90 miles away. It came time to go home, but Pop-Pop was in no condition to drive. He'd had far too much to drink. So guess who drove home from Lewistown, at night, before there were highways to make the driving straight and easy?

That's right.

Thirteen-year-old Elam.

And when Elam was old enough to drive and found a way to buy a car, his father became even more desperate to get to local watering holes. Pop-Pop even took Elam's keys from time to time. Wrecked a couple of Elam's cars. It was bad.

Elam wasn't the only one driving for his father. When Barbie was 13 years old (this would have been years after Elam's drive home from Lewistown), Pop-Pop convinced her and her friend to go with him in the pick-up truck. He pulled into the parking lot outside a local bar.

"No, Pop! Not now. Not there."

"C'mon," he insisted. "Let's go in. You can get a soda."

They sat there with him at the bar for hours as he had drink after drink. He became more and more intoxicated. They kept nagging him to go home, so he threw the keys to Barbie.

"Go on. Take a spin," he said, wanting to get rid of them and their complaining. "Just leave me be."

So Barbie and her friend drove the pick-up around Leola, cruising the back roads, wasting time. After an hour or so, they drove back to the bar, picked up Pop-Pop, and then drove him home.

Perhaps the important thing to remember is that while all of this was going on, they were still Amish! Pop-Pop almost always had a vehicle, something that made his father-in-law very unhappy and had him in constant trouble with the Amish church. But his rebellious behavior didn't only affect himself – it also had a huge affect on his children and the kind of life it made for them.

As my dad and his brothers and sisters grew older, Pop-Pop seemed to get further and further off track. The older children walked into church on a Sunday morning, surrounded by their Amish community. (Amish church is held in one of the member's homes, a different place each week. The men sit on one side, the women and children on the other.) When the Lapp family walked into the house and navigated the benches, the whispering began.

Naomi especially remembers hearing the mumblings about her father. None of the little girls her age wanted to talk to her or play with her. That's just the way it was, and it didn't change as she grew older – in fact, it got worse. For a teenager not to be accepted by her peers because of what her dad was doing, that hurt. When she hit her teenage years, she didn't have many boys asking her out because their parents didn't want their sons going on a date with Christ Lapp's daughter. He was trouble. They didn't want anything to do with him.

While their father made life difficult, their mother was

the complete opposite.

"She was an angel from above," Elam says, and all the children echo that sentiment. They all have wonderful memories of Rachel, including how she would come out and help them milk the cows in the morning, going in just early enough to get breakfast ready for everyone. Or how she drove a disc with four mules in front of her. Or how she tended the huge garden they had.

Rachel was full of love for her children, even when, one by one, they left the Amish.

Which is exactly what Naomi did in May of 1959.

Chapter Seven
Leaving the Amish

Recently I sat with my dad's sisters and heard their stories.

"I went downstairs to tell Mom I was leaving," Naomi recalled. "It was about 5 or 6 in the morning, and I had to tell her because I had a haircut appointment that afternoon, and I wanted her to know."

"I told her, 'Mom, I'm leaving the Amish,' and she looked at me with tears in her eyes and said, 'Whatever makes you happy.' That's all she said. 'Whatever makes you happy.' That's just the kind of mom she was. Then we both cried and hugged, and she never once scolded me. She was a saint until the day she died. She was always there for me. Always."

Because my aunt Naomi left the Amish after she had joined the church, she was shunned. Later, when Pop-Pop left, he and my grandmother Rachel would be shunned as

36

well. None of the other siblings ever joined the church, so when they drifted away from the Amish, they weren't shunned.

It's hard to explain how shunning creates these invisible walls between people. It's hard to explain the impact this would have on the family in the coming years.

Always as a counterweight to Pop-Pop's anger and drinking was their mother Rachel's kindness. None of the children ever remember her yelling or getting upset with them. In fact, when Christy was 12 or 13, a few of the boys who lived across the street wanted him to go hang out with them. He was pretty determined to go along, even though they were trouble.

"I don't think you should go," his mother said.

He complained, he whined, he argued. She never raised her voice, but she continued insisting.

"I don't think you should go, Christy."

Finally, reluctantly, he gave in. He would stay home, not because he wanted to, but because he didn't want to disappoint his mother. Later that day, those boys ended up getting caught robbing a convenience store, and Christy escaped the punishment because he didn't go along.

Or perhaps it would be more accurate to say that Christy escaped the punishment because of his mother.

Then there was the time Barbie was invited to go on

vacation with a friend of hers. The problem was that this friend wasn't Amish. Well, her mom took her out and bought her all new non-Amish clothes so that when she went on vacation she wouldn't feel out of place.

"She was the coolest mom ever," Barbie said. "When I got home from that trip, she sat and listened while I told her every single thing we did. She couldn't get enough. That's always how Mom was – she wanted to hear about everything us kids did, and she'd listen to us go on and on about anything."

In the late 50s and early 60s, things got worse with Pop-Pop. Sometimes he got loud with his wife Rachel, sometimes on the edge of mean. By then, my dad Manny was old enough to stand up to him, and he'd step in, protect his own mother, keep Pop-Pop in line. Some of my aunts and uncles described some pretty intense scenes in the house.

One Christmas Eve, Pop-Pop hadn't come home from the bar, and I guess my dad had just about had enough. Christmas Eve was always a family time, and everyone was disappointed that Pop-Pop wasn't there, so my dad went looking for him. My dad drove from bar to bar, and when he finally found him, he hauled him out and shoved him into the car. Pop-Pop kept fighting him to get out of the car and back into the bar. My dad held him in his seat the whole way back, and coming in the driveway, Pop-Pop broke off the sun visor trying to escape the car.

After Dad had successfully retrieved Pop-Pop, someone else went to pick up Aunt Mary and bring her over to the house. That's when Pop-Pop started crying because he didn't want his sister, his only living sibling, to see him that way. It was like a switch with him – one moment he was angry and in your face; the next moment he was a heap of tears on the floor, crying about who he had become.

In the Amish church, if you break the rules, you have to show you are penitent by sitting up front beside the bishop, the deacon, and the preachers. You have to keep your head bowed down for the entire service as a sign of your penitence. Because of the things Pop-Pop did, like drinking or keeping a car hidden for his own use, he spent almost every single church day sitting up beside the bishops, his head down.

No matter what Pop-Pop did during the week, he still showed up on Sunday for church. Maybe this is because one of the preachers was his father-in-law, or maybe he had become so used to the discipline that it didn't bother him anymore. He sat up front and took the punishment. Aunt Lydia remembers seeing my father in church crying because of all these things that happened to his own father. She remembers how the other children treated them outside, after church was over.

"Your dad's never around," the other kids hissed at the

Lapp children. "He drinks. He's a bad man."

In the early 60s, things pretty much hit rock bottom. Pop-Pop ended up going to jail twice for behavior related to his drinking. The first time it was a minor thing, just an overnight visit to jail, but for the second offense, he had to serve time in prison for one year. One year away from the family. One year behind bars. His head and beard were shaved.

It was then that he was excommunicated from the Amish church.

In the midst of that trying time, a few of my aunts and uncles remember their mother Rachel piling all the kids into a car and driving them somewhere. She went into the city and turned onto Broad Street, went over a bridge, and stopped the car. She pointed up the hill, behind the "poor house," and there was their dad, wearing prison garb, working for the state on a large farming plot where the prison took non-violent offenders to work while they served their time. They waved to him, and he saw them and waved back.

Once again, Rachel held the family together. Many mothers would have left my pop-pop, or tried to get away, but my Grandmother Rachel took the kids to see him. How desperately she wanted her family to stay together.

Most of the children had already left the Amish on their own by the time Pop-Pop left the Amish church in 1963 (my dad left the Amish when he was 16 years old, in 1959). Things changed quickly. All Pop-Pop had to do in order to keep the farm was remain Amish, but with his excommunication, he lost all of that, and the family had to move to a smaller place over on Mt. Sidney Road in Witmer. He went from being a farmer to working as a stone mason. They started attending a small Brethren Church.

He was the town drunk of Bird-in-Hand, and the children, now teenagers, continued to be bullied and put down by Amish kids who knew about it. And because there was a void there, because there was no active father in place, the kids started looking to my dad, their brother Manny. They didn't disrespect Pop-Pop, and they stopped looking to him for answers.

For some families, this would have ruined them. Many children who grow up in such a dysfunctional environment struggle to get their own lives in order. Many children of alcoholics follow in the same pattern.

But not my dad. He was determined to live a different life than the one he had experienced.

As a friend of my father's told me, "Manny and I grew up with the same situation: we both had a father who drank. We had nothing given to us. If we were going to have anything in life, we were going to have to find it ourselves. Manny knew he couldn't follow in his father's footsteps and attain anything in life. He grew up with nothing, but he wanted to be something."

That's what my dad did. He went out and he made something of himself.

This is in the meadow at the family farm, sometime around 1945. Pop-Pop and Mom-Mom are with their three oldest children: Aunt Naomi, Uncle Elam, and my dad, Manny.

Pop-Pop and Mom-Mom with the five youngest children: Aunt Feenie,
Aunt Anna Mary, Uncle Wilmer, Aunt Barbi, and Uncle Christy

The six oldest siblings stand in front of the farmhouse.

Attending a non-Amish wedding for friends of the family, the Brians.
Back left to right: Naomi, Manny, and Elam
Front right to left: Wilmer (on Mrs. Brian's lap), Feenie, and Anna Mary

Willow Road one-room schoolhouse.
That's my dad Manny marked with the star.

My dad (left) with his brother Elam, around 1953.

The bouvas (PA Dutch for "boys") softball team. Manny is at the top left, Wilmer is below him with his hand on his knee, Elam is in the center left holding the cake, Jay Hershey (first Lapp Electric employee) is in the center next to Elam, and Christy is the young guy holding his ears.

49

Naomi's wedding day (1966)
Left to right: Christy, Wilmer, Manny, Elam, Pop-Pop, Mom-Mom, Naomi,
Feenie, Anna Mary, and Barbi.

My dad in his typical Lapp electric uniform.

Mom-Mom, Pop-Pop, my dad (in the tuxedo), and all my aunts and uncles at Marisa and I's wedding reception.

*To Marisa and Tim Lapp
With best wishes,*

Hanging out with President George W. Bush when he visited Lapp Electric
in July, 2004. Take a look at mom and dad smiling.
That was an awesome day.

Mom-Mom and Pop-Pop Lapp.

My parents, Manny and Flossie Lapp: a gift to me from God.

My favorite picture of Dad and me.

The Lapper coin we created to honor my dad.

PART TWO

SHINING

For the Blessings That Remain
By Elam Stoltzfoos

There are loved ones who are missing,
From the fireside and the feast.
There are faces who have vanished,
There are voices that have ceased.
But you know they passed forever,
From our mortal grief and pain.
But we thank Thee Our Father,
For the Blessings that remain.

Thanksgiving, Oh Thanksgiving,
That their love once blessed us here.
That so long they walked beside us,
Sharing every smile and tear.
For the joy the past has brought us,
But can never take away.
For the sweet and precious memories,
Growing dearer every day.

For the faith that keeps us patient,
Looking at the things unseen.
Knowing spring shall follow winter,
And the earth again be green.
For the hope of that glad meeting,
Far from mortal grief and pain.
We thank Thee Our Father,
For the Blessings that remain.

Chapter Eight
The First Amish Electrician

Determined to make a life for himself that was better than the life his father had given him, Manny got his first job as a young Amish boy. He was only 12 or 13 years old when he started working at Landy Towel and Linen, a company responsible for taking deliveries of dirty industrial towels and uniforms, washing them, and delivering the clean ones.

They backed trucks up to their docks and opened the rear gates. The stench was horrific! My dad crawled into the trucks filled with used towels and aprons and threw everything out so it could be collected and washed. He was a hard worker, and that was his introduction into life as an employee.

After that, about the time he turned 16, he drove a milk truck for Jack Robinson in Bird-in-Hand. I'm not sure if he kept the job at Landy Towel or not, but I do know that for most of his young life he worked two or three jobs simultaneously.

My father's good friend Duane Reitz met my dad in 1957.

"In our conversations together," Duane recently told me, "it was clear that we both had ambitions to advance ourselves in life to something more challenging, something more financially rewarding. In those days, Manny studied electrical books every chance he had. He taught himself the basics of electricity."

While my dad took those years as an opportunity to start working and saving his money, his own father didn't change much, if at all. Jay Hershey, one of my dad's best friends and the very first employee at Lapp Electric, remembers pulling into the house one day only to be greeted by my grandmother Rachel as she came running out the door.

"You've got to stop him!" she shouted. "You can't let him drive away like this!"

Pop-Pop was drunker than a skunk, and he came stumbling through the door towards his truck.

"I'll get the keys," Jay said.

Pop-Pop heard him and lurched over to the porch where he grabbed a .22 rifle and turned it on Jay. That was a tense moment, but Jay somehow managed to take the gun and usher Pop-Pop back inside. Rachel followed close after, and once they were all through the door, she pushed Pop-Pop over the coffee table, and he landed on the couch, where he promptly went to sleep.

Another friend of my father's remembers driving through Leola early one morning before anyone else was on the road. Pop-Pop's pick-up truck was parked in the middle of the road, and when my dad's friend got out to see what was going on, he found Pop-Pop asleep against the steering wheel. My dad's friend pushed the truck over into the bank and put the keys on the seat. He also opened all the windows, hoping the freezing cold winter air would help him to sober up.

He drove away. I can't help but wonder how many people in the community have similar stories about Pop-Pop that we've never heard.

My dad was young when he met my mother, Flossie, during a dance at the Manheim Township Park. I don't know many of the details of their courtship or early years as a married couple, but that's where they met.

My dad's friends have said that to them, he was "Manny," but to Flossie, he was always "EMANUEL!" It seemed she was always shouting his name for one reason or another.

But they also remember her as a kind wife, who always had a tray of cinnamon rolls ready for the guys before they left for work in the morning or a cherry pie waiting for anyone who joined Manny at home for lunch.

My dad's job as a maintenance man at High Steel seems to have moved him in the direction of being an electrician more than anything else in his life. His job involved doing some electrical work, and he was intrigued by it. He started a small side business, a little shop behind the house, where he tinkered with appliances if people needed to have them fixed.

Once he realized he wanted to have a business of his own, he started looking for a loan to cover the cost of getting started. In 1968 and 1969, he approached three different banks. But in those first attempts, he was not successful. The banks wouldn't give him the money, and each of the bank managers gave him the same reason: "You're Christ Lapp's son."

Even then, nearly a decade after leaving the Amish church, Pop-Pop's legacy was still impacting his children for the worse.

The fourth bank my father went to, they gave him an opportunity, and he never forgot that. It started out as the Bank of Lancaster County, and the name has changed over the years, but that was his bank, and he stuck with them.

Chapter Nine

"An Amish Man Can't Do Electric"

He started Lapp Electrical Service, Inc. in 1969, the year before us twin boys were born and the year after my brother Greg was born. In the beginning, it was a one-man show. But business was good, and he needed to pick up an employee, preferably someone with a little more electrical experience than he had himself.

Whenever my dad drove through the little village of Witmer, he would stop by Jay Hershey's house. Jay was one of my dad's brother Wilmer's friends, but the three of them had spent a fair amount of time together. At one point, the three of them had gone up to the inn at Bridgeport after getting a call that Pop-Pop was causing problems. They drove Pop-Pop's blue and white International pick-up and took a length of rope, and when they found him, they tied him up and threw him in the back of the truck until he sobered up.

Well, my dad kept bothering Jay about joining him in his business. He knew that Jay worked over at Ross Engineering, where he did industrial and commercial electrical work.

My dad would go flying in the lane and shout out to Jay, "I've got a job for you," but Jay kept putting him off.

Finally, my dad stopped in one evening on his way home from work.

"Like I said, I've got a job for you," Manny said. "Are you gonna work for me or not? I'm not stopping again – call me by tonight."

Jay called him that night and started working for my dad two days before my twin brother and I were born. Jay worked for Lapp Electrical Services for the next 42 years, only retiring a few years ago.

My dad's brother Christy also worked for him that first summer. And sometimes Pop-Pop would tag along.

"Dumb thing isn't going to work anyway," Pop-Pop said on more than one occasion about work my dad was doing. "Everyone knows an Amish man can't do electric."

But, contrary to what "everyone" knew, my dad could do electric. He could do it well. He always looked at it as a service, not just a business, and he'd bend over backwards to help out his customers. Nothing gets people talking about a company faster than extraordinary service.

For example, one night the owner of a local company contacted Dad with an emergency: his well pump didn't work, and he was wondering if Manny would come out and take a look at it. Well, it was the middle of the night, but my dad, as usual, said yes.

"I'm not a plumber, but I'll take a look at it."

He and Jay went down there and fooled around with it and you know what? They fixed that well pump. It was a call most other electricians would have declined before rolling over and going back to sleep. But not my dad. And you know what? Taking that call led to millions of dollars of electrical work with that same company through the years.

There was another middle-of-the-night call that makes me smile. My dad showed up alone to a house late one evening. The lady who was there showed him the problem and watched him while he worked. I guess he asked her to hold one of his tools, and she stuck it in her bra. When he asked for the tool back, she leaned in and suggested he take it himself.

My dad must have felt kind of guilty about the whole thing because he told my mom about it. She got really upset, and she told Jay that "if there are any more night time calls, you're going!"

But you know what? People found out that if you called Manny or one of his key employees, no matter what time of the day or night, they'd show up. That's something that's been passed down to the next generation of Lapp men, and I can't say it's always a positive thing. Sometimes we'll do as much as we can for our customers, even if our family is put on the back burner because of it. But that customers-first attitude is definitely what grew the company in the early days.

My mom had to put up with that a lot when it came to middle-of-the-night or early-morning phone calls. One morning at 4am, two of my dad's employees were ready and waiting for my dad to go to a job. When he didn't show up, they had a little argument over whose responsibility it was to call the house.

"You should call him!" the one employee said.

"I ain't calling him this early," the second employee said.

"Fine."

So the first employee called the house. Flossie answered, and she let him have it for calling so early.

"Don't ever call here at this time again!" she said.

"Hey, don't yell at me," the employee said calmly. "Yell at that guy beside you in bed."

Chapter Ten
Flossie

In my earliest memories of my dad, he is working or coming home from work in his Lapp Electric gear. In the 80s, that would have been a green Lapp Electric baseball cap, a gray, long-sleeved shirt with an American flag patch on his left shoulder, and blue jeans.

During those busy first years, my mom Flossie really kept our family together. Dad was leaving early and coming home late, and Mom took care of us boys on her own for many hours out of the week.

One morning, Duane Reitz arrived at our home to deliver some heating oil for the house.

"As I got out of the truck," Duane said, "Flossie came out of the house and asked me if I had seen her twin boys. Tim's twin brother suddenly appeared and told Flossie that his brother was in the basement, so I went down to help her look for Tim."

"Well, we got down there and Flossie asked where Tim was. His brother pointed at the refrigerator, Flossie opened the door, and out came four-year-old Tim."

As I got older, Mom was the one who helped me get through the hardships of growing up, the rejection and teenage angst. Mom was always the shoulder to cry on, and then she'd build me up.

Her kindness was stretched in the mornings though as she was also the one given the unenviable task of waking up us three boys.

"Boys!" she shouted in her piercing voice. "Get up!"

My mom was also involved in the business, albeit in a "consulting role." She was the bookkeeper. My dad was the nice one, friends to everyone, and my mom was the hard-nosed business woman. She was the mean one. She was the one who tracked people down and made them pay their bills. She was the one who pressured my dad to get rid of employees who weren't pulling their own weight. She held everyone, *everyone*, to a high standard.

Her dedication and kindness to me as a young man more than made up for my dad being away so much.

I think these are traits my grandmother and my mother both had. They had a way of stepping in and taking up the slack. My grandmother shielded the kids as best she could from the affects of her husband's alcoholism, and I think my mom shielded us boys as best she could from the affects of my dad's busy-ness. It takes a certain dedication and intense focus to grow a business, and my dad had that. He was willing to put in the hours, and my mom was willing to support him in that.

Both my grandmother and my mother were strong, wonderful women, and as the years have passed, I see that I chose a wife with the same strength and grace.

Where my mom is now, well, it's a difficult place. She was diagnosed as having dementia with Alzheimer's, and it's been a tough road for the family. I just saw her a few days ago, and it takes some time to think through it. The most difficult thing I've had to do is to look at my mom and realize she's not there anymore. The mom I grew up with is fading away.

My kids, my wife, and I went on Saturday to see her, and when we knocked on her door and went in, she looked at us with a blank look. She didn't recognize us at first.

"Hey, Mom," I said.

This is the part of the journey we're on, though it's certainly not an easy part. But this is the way we move from one generation to the next, with as much kindness and grace as we can muster. It's all part of the story.

Chapter Eleven
Intervention

In the 70s, the business grew to around ten employees, and in the 80s, things started to take off. It got larger, and my dad added even more people, taking on contract work for large construction companies.

Our company grew because of the demand. My dad worked beside his employees for 60 or 70 hours a week, and when it got too busy, he'd say, "I'd better get another truck," or "Time to hire another employee." It was an organic growth based entirely on an inability to keep up.

But the real reason the Lapp Electrical Services got as large as it did was because my dad did not shy away from hiring employees who knew more than he did. Every employee was encouraged to operate in their areas of strength. For example, at one point, my dad hired Jimmy Bailey, a guy who knew a lot about the commercial and industrial end of electrical work. My dad let him take off into work they had not previously been involved in, or at least not to that extent, and Jimmy grew the business in those areas.

Along with giving employees that kind of freedom, he also never came down hard on their mistakes. This combination of letting people loose and giving them the freedom to fail led to an explosion of growth at the company.

Growing up in that kind of an environment, where the company was growing so fast, my brothers and I found ourselves entering into a situation of forced labor. That's just how it was. My dad had us digging ditches in the summer, running conduit, and doing whatever non-skilled work he could find for us to do. The grunt work. We were probably around 12 or 13 years old when he pulled us into working for the company. The first job I had was waking up at 6am on Saturday mornings to wash the Lapp Electric trucks.

Washing the trucks was a Saturday event that I never looked forward to, but you know what? I'm still doing it to this day. Now I share the responsibility with my brother Greg, so every other weekend my kids and I wash the trucks. I think it helps my own kids learn a small lesson in taking responsibility. I think it helped me (although I certainly didn't appreciate it at the time).

In 1984, my dad continued his entrepreneurial ways by building the second self-storage business in Lancaster, PA. It began with 88 units, and as the years passed, he added another 280 climate-controlled units as well as commercial office space.

My dad was always looking for ways to grow the business, and in the early 90s, he was asked by a loyal and valued customer of Lapp Electric if he would like to partner with him on a commercial property. This man was a multimillionaire who owned a beautiful horse farm in Bird-In-Hand, PA. He asked my dad to find a property in Lancaster that would be a good investment and get back to him. This was like the modern day *Shark Tank* for my dad.

Manny invested $10,000, and the other gentleman offered up some collateral to become 50/50 partners with my dad in what would become Triple J Mobile Home Park in Gordonville, PA.

In 1969, it was Lapp Electric. In the early 80s, it was East End Storage. In the early 90s, it was Triple J. After that, he established a Family Limited Partnership called East End Enterprises for my two brothers and I to be partners. My dad created an empire for my brothers and I to sustain, maintain, and grow, and of course the pressure is always there not to screw it up!

Through all of these years and businesses and challenges, my dad never blamed his dad for his misfortunes or used him as an excuse. He loved his dad and turned the negative into a positive. He would not let the sins of his father keep him down.

Reaching adulthood doesn't mean the problems of your past simply disappear. Just because my dad had started a successful business and a family didn't mean his own father had changed all that much or magically managed to escape the demons of his past.

For weeks Pop-Pop would lay on the sofa and not eat. He was depressed for months at a time, and he fought his depression the only way he knew how: he chased it to the bottom of the bottle.

Then, after weeks of depression, living in the haze of a drunken stupor, he'd wake up one morning at 4am and walk to the store, suddenly feeling fine. That's how obvious it was when he rose up out of those lows. The highs, those periods between severe depressions, were obvious and fast paced. Energetic. The kids, grown and out of the house by now, had a simple way of talking about Pop-Pop's quick recoveries.

"Pop woke up," they'd say, shrugging their shoulders, unable to explain it.

Finally, Pop-Pop's children decided to try and do something about their father's drinking. My own mother Flossie initiated it and arranged for my Grandmother Rachel to bring Pop-Pop to a certain place. I'm not sure what she told him in order to get him there, but they showed up at a counseling service somewhere in the west end of Lancaster. My grandmother walked Pop-Pop into a room where all of his children were waiting for him.

At first, once Pop-Pop realized what was happening, he was angry.

"Do you know why we're here?" the counselor asked Pop-Pop.

Pop-Pop nodded, so angry he could barely talk. The counselor continued.

"I'd like to start by going around the room and having everyone say one thing that makes you sad your father is an alcoholic."

One by one, each of his children said one thing that saddened them. Barbie, the daughter who used to be too embarrassed by her father to invite her friends to her house, spoke softly.

This was the same Barbie who remembered her father getting ready to go to the American Legion in Lewistown when she was a little girl. Her mom would go along with him, bringing all the children, because she didn't want him going by himself and didn't want to leave the children home alone. Those little Amish kids, including Barbie, sat in the car by themselves for hours. Their mother kept coming out and checking on them while their father sat in at the bar and became increasingly intoxicated. At some point, he would come back out, and their mother would drive them all home. The only reason she went along was because she didn't want him driving home when he was drunk, and they couldn't afford the cab fare for such a long trip.

With those memories pressing to the forefront of her mind, Barbie said what made her sad about her father's alcoholism.

"I don't want my kids to grow up and see you that way," she said, her voice trembling with emotion.

As each of his children spoke, Pop-Pop wept. The long-standing remorse he felt turned into action, and after that intervention a lot of things changed, the main one being his regular attendance at AA meetings.

Chapter Twelve
Reunited

Ever since I was a little kid, I knew my father respected and loved me, but he didn't say it often. He wasn't verbally encouraging, probably because he never received that from his own father. But he loved me. Somehow, I always knew that.

Maybe it was in the way he made time for us, even when the business demanded so much. Back in 1986, during the summer between 10th and 11th grade, Dad took us all on a cross-country RV trip. We went and saw the Grand Canyon, Disney Land, San Francisco, Mount Rushmore, and then we came home. It lasted about a month, but when I think about it, that was a big deal back then. Thirty days off? Without cell phones or computers? My dad took a month away from his business to spend that time with us.

I graduated from Conestoga Valley High School in 1988, and at that point, there were around 30 employees at Lapp Electric. The 90s were booming and the company grew to nearly 70 people and around $6 million in revenue.

I graduated from college in 1992 and went straight into the family business. In January of 1993, as a sort of celebration of my graduation, Dad took me out to Yellowstone National Park, and we went snowmobiling. Ron Martin came along, a good friend of my dad's, as well as my cousin Shane and Uncle Tom. What an incredible experience.

We drove 50 miles or more every single day on snowmobiles, flying through that wide-open country. What an awesome memory. I long to go back. I loved experiencing the overwhelming sense that I was in God's country.

The snow stretched out in every direction, and the horizon was always lined with snow-capped mountains. It was unbelievably quiet and peaceful. I remember the humming of the massive transformers when we shut off our engines. The snowflakes drifted down around us, and my breath came and went in cloudy bursts. What an experience.

There was one stretch where our guide told us we could open it up, and for two or three miles, we flew along at 80 mph. It was so freeing.

At night we'd bunk up together, the four of us, and I shared a bed with my dad. We all smoked at the time, and the motel room was full of smoke as we rehashed each day's

81

adventures.

When we got back, I found my way around the family business, and in 1994, I moved into the office. That was also the year I got married. First I worked in accounts payable doing data entry. In 1995, I became more involved in the storage business Dad owned. I managed that for about ten years. It was my introduction to working for my dad in an official capacity, and it seemed to go pretty well.

My grandmother Rachel went into the hospital with stomach pains in 1996, and they soon realized she had a twisted bowel. There was nothing they could do. She would never survive surgery on the bowel – her heart was too weak. She was in a lot of pain, so much pain in fact that she had a button she could push to self-administer morphine every so often.

"Christy," she asked her youngest son in a weak voice, "Could you please hit the button?"

Someone was with her all the time.

At some point during that last week, Christy drove over to see Rachel's older brother Levi. Levi had stayed Amish all those years, and he had barely spoken to his sister since the early 60s, when Rachel had been torn away from the Amish by her husband, my pop-pop. This is the sad part of Amish shunning, when families are split in half, when brothers and sisters barely speak to each other for decades.

To be honest, I didn't know much about shunning until just before my pop-pop died. During one of the last years of my grandfather's life, my dad and I took him along to Bird-in-Hand Restaurant to meet with some of my dad's business friends, who just happened to be Amish.

"You know," my dad said when he arrived, "Pop-Pop can't sit at the same table as the rest of those Amish men today."

"What?" I asked. "I have no idea what you're talking about."

"He's shunned by the Amish. They won't sit with him."

I thought my dad was losing his mind – it sounded ludicrous to me! But when we sat down with these Amish men, our table was made up of two separate tables situated about an inch apart. They brought the one table to within an inch of the other table, but because they weren't touching, that was enough to satisfy the rule that the Amish men not eat with someone who had been shunned from the Amish.

What the heck is this? I thought to myself. *My grandfather is 89 years old, and he can't sit at the same table as you?*

I had a really hard time with that. It was one of the strangest things I've ever seen, but I didn't want to offend or insult the Amish men, so I didn't say anything. Later I found out more – not only could my pop-pop not eat at the same table as Amish people in "good standing" with the Amish church, they also wouldn't accept cash directly from him. If he wanted to pay an Amish person, he'd have to lay the money down on the counter for them to pick up or give it to someone else to hand to them. I was flabbergasted.

My father, on the other hand, wasn't shunned by the Amish because he left before officially joining the church.

Anyway, as my grandmother lay dying, Christy went into Levi's house, and they spoke for a few minutes. Then he brought up Rachel.

"This is your last chance," Christy told Levi. "If you want to see your sister before she dies, now is the time."

Levi sat there in silence, considering this Amish ritual of shunning for a few moments before nodding his head. He wanted to see Rachel. He had seen her a few years before that at one of her birthday parties. His youngest brother Wilmer had driven over to his house to invite him to go along.

"We should go to our sister's birthday party," Wilmer had told Levi.

"They left us," Levi had said in a matter-of-fact voice. "We're not on the same page as them anymore."

"I know that," Wilmer said, "and you don't have to agree with everybody in order to visit them and love them."

"I can't go," Levi said again.

"Levi," Wilmer implored him. "if Rachel dies before you, will you go to her funeral?"

Silence.

"I probably would," Levi admitted.

"Well, then you should go and visit her while she's still living."

Maybe Levi had those words in mind years later when he went to pay a visit to his dying sister. Christy drove Levi to the hospital, and they both made the long trek through the hallways and up the elevator to Rachel's room.

Levi walked in, and as soon as he saw his sister and she saw him, they both started crying. Pop-Pop's alcoholism had hurt the family and led to years of dysfunction, starting with the division of his wife's own family.

Levi apologized to her that day, when she was dying, said he was sorry he had let everything come between them. Everyone felt bad that so much time had been missed.

Rachel lived for a few more days.

"The day mother passed away was the saddest thing I ever experienced up to that point," her daughter Barbie says. "The last time I saw her was in the hospital before she died. One or two of us stayed with her every single night. Wilmer and I were there with her, and I said, 'Mother, smile for me one time.' I didn't think she could hear me, but she smiled. We spent the last few hours singing old hymns for her. Then she was gone."

Chapter Thirteen
Changing Times

It seems that even the hardest hearts can change after enough time passes. It makes me wonder how my thinking about someone might change once decades have gone by.

After my grandmother died, Pop-Pop asked Elam to drive him down to Christiana to see his sister Mary's house. Mary was still Amish after all these years. Elam drove Pop-Pop down there, and Pop-Pop told him to park at the end of the long lane.

"Should we drive in and say hello?" Elam asked Pop-Pop.

Pop-Pop just held up his hand and stared down the lane. "No," he said, "I don't think I want to go in."

So they sat there, the car engine off. After a time, Pop-Pop leaned back in the car seat and sighed.

"Okay," he told Elam. "Let's go."

And they drove away.

Sometimes Pop-Pop would go visit his brother-in-law, Rachel's younger brother Wilmer, who had one time had been the little boy straining to see through the window, trying hard to see who this man was who was taking his sister away. Rachel had passed away by then, so the two brother-in-laws sat and talked about the weather, the farm, the community. Wilmer lived on the farm where my grandmother Rachel had grown up…the Stoltzfoos Family farm.

Pop-Pop would often talk to Wilmer about how he had hurt Wilmer's parents.

"I was a bad boy," he said in a quiet voice. "I was a bad boy."

There would be tears in his eyes when he said it.

"I have some regrets, Wilmer. Will you pray for me?"

So Wilmer said a prayer for Pop-Pop. This is what time can do. This is how time can change things.

In 1998, at around 7am on a Sunday morning, our phone rang. I answered, wondering what someone could possibly want at that hour on a weekend.

It was my pop-Pop, and he was extremely sad. At first I couldn't understand what he was saying.

"Pop-Pop, is everything okay?" I asked him.

I realized he was crying.

"Wilmer was killed," he managed to say between sobs.

"You mean great-uncle Wilmer?" I asked him, thinking that he must be referring to his wife Rachel's brother. The one who had once been a little boy watching for Pop-Pop to arrive.

"No," he said, and after another long silence, he managed to choke out two words.

"My son."

My uncle Wilmer was dead. My father's brother. We were, all of us, shocked and devastated.

During the last several years of my Pop-Pop's life, he would often share with me the same words.

"A father should never have to bury his son."

Life isn't always what we expect it to be. There is joy and heartache, good news and bad news, happiness and despair. We've had our mix of it, to be sure. But we face it together as a family, and that means a lot.

Mom, Dad, and my wife Marisa, they all came to me in the early 2000s and said they thought I needed more of a challenge. Their encouragement got me more involved in Lapp Electric, and then in 2002, shortly after my father's leukemia diagnosis, my brother Greg and I bought Dad out of the business.

Something that happened soon after that kind of put us on the map. People knew about Lapp Electric, but when the President of the United States comes to your business, people pay attention.

In 2004, a friend of my wife called me up. He worked for the Republican National Committee. While we were on vacation he called me and said he put our name in a hat to host a visit from the President. He wasn't sure if anything would come of it, but if we were chosen, he wondered if we were interested in having President Bush come and visit our company.

"Is the pope Catholic?" I asked him.

Some people called and interviewed my brother and I. Then, we found out President George W. Bush was coming to visit Lapp Electric. There's a photo I have of the family with President Bush, and my dad, he has this overjoyed look on his face. It was a real highlight for him to see this company he had built from the ground up in 1969 hosting the President of the United States 35 years later.

The day was wild. We had a marketing company come out and help us promote the event all week. Just about every day that week, we were in the newspaper. A CNN truck pulled up outside and parked beside the NBC truck. Secret Service guys were on the roof. We had to move stuff out of the warehouse in order to accommodate the crowd of 250 people. It was a day I'll never forget.

"These are the Lapp boys," the President said at one point in his speech. "They took over their dad's business. Manny and his wife are here today. Isn't it great when sons follow in their father's footsteps?"

After his speech, he came up to the conference room and hung out with us and our newest employee. We had hired six people that year and the President was on the campaign trail talking about small businesses and how important they were to the economy. Later, I gave him a hard time about being a Cowboys fan (I'm a Redskins fan).

My brother and I had co-owned the business for two years at that point. In those early days, I was trying to earn my place in the eyes of the employees, trying to earn their respect. I even spent the first year out in the field, trying to build relationships with the guys I worked with. After that, I went out and tried to earn the respect of the customers. But now, it's coming back around again, and the older I get the more I recognize the cycle.

Chapter Fourteen
Shunning to Shining

When Pop-Pop collapsed and died on January 13th, 2010, my father was also in the hospital. He had been diagnosed with leukemia ten years prior, and for the four years leading up to January of 2010, he had not been doing well. The doctors recommended that my father have a bone marrow transplant, so the whole family took blood tests to see if anyone could be a donor.

There was only one close match.

His oldest brother Elam. The same Elam who had hidden in the back of the runaway buggy, the same Elam who had driven his father 100 miles home from Lewistown when he was just a kid, the same Elam who had shot his sister Naomi in the butt with a BB gun.

Elam and his wife went along with my parents, Manny and Flossie, to John Hopkins Hospital the day before the scheduled transfusion and spent the night. Then, they went in early the next morning and had a few more last-minute tests done to make sure Elam wasn't sick. They tested just about everything they could test to make sure his marrow was in a suitable state to give to Manny because my father was so sick that any kind of infection, no matter how small, would have devastated his system.

They put Elam under, drew the blood out of his bone marrow, and took it right over to Manny. I can't think of something that exemplifies a man's love for his brother more than what Elam did for my father that day. Elam returned home at night, but Manny stayed down for what ended up being several months as the doctors tried to coax his body back to health.

"It was the greatest thing I could ever do," Elam says with tears in his eyes. "It was awesome. Awesome. I was very fortunate and blessed that I could be the donor."

After the bone marrow transplant, Manny aged tremendously. He started getting sores on his face from where his skin was peeling away. The thing that was incredible about my dad was that, even in the midst of recovering from a bone marrow transplant, even after fighting leukemia, he never complained. He wouldn't talk about his cancer or his treatment, not even if you asked him about it. He worked hard to get on with life, and if you brought up his illness, he'd change the subject before you knew what happened.

Not only did he rarely complain – he kept showing up at random places to help people!

For example, one day he took his tractor to a house one of his siblings had just bought. "The first thing we're going to do is get rid of these bushes," Manny said, and he proceeded to pull out all of the bushes with his tractor. He was drinking his favorite tea and covered in bandages from where his skin wouldn't heal. He just about ran over his brother Elam with the backhoe, but he was in his glory, working hard, making progress.

"Those last years with Manny," one of my dad's friends tells me, "I'll never forget them. I went to visit him at his house before he died, and we sat there on the couch, remembering old times. Out of Manny's appreciation, he gave me some money, and as he handed it to me, he said, 'This is for you. I don't care what you do with it.'"

"I couldn't help but ask myself, *What would Manny do with this money?* I remembered there was a relief sale going on nearby, so I went over and gave the money on behalf of Manny."

That was one of the incredible things about my dad. He instilled the knowledge in everyone around him that it's not about us – it's about everyone else.

My father faded considerably during that last month. He

wasn't doing well at all. By the time Pop-Pop died, my dad couldn't even go to the viewing or funeral. I was with my dad every day that week after Pop-Pop died. Every day. I spent the night with him when he first went in to the hospital. That last week he spent here on Earth, he was in and out of consciousness. I'm not sure how aware he was of everything that was going on.

The day after Pop-Pop's funeral, my dad's brother Elam traveled down to Texas for a week. It wasn't but a few days later that my brother Greg called him with the sad news that my dad was on his way home as well. So Elam hopped back on to a plane and flew to Pennsylvania.

"Manny waited for Elam," Naomi said. "He got there around midnight the night before Manny died, and it seemed like after that he was really on his way out, as if he had wanted to see Elam one last time before he died."

Did you know that some people refer to that third Monday in January as Blue Monday? There's not any science behind it, but it's purported to be the saddest day of the year. It was at 7am on that Blue Monday in January of 2010 that the nurses came into where I was sitting with my brothers Geoff and Greg at the bedside of our father.

"You should probably go get your mother," they said. "We don't think your father has much time left."

After the nurses told us that dad was on his way out, I

hopped in the car and drove home as fast as I could to pick up Mom. We got back, and he had passed away about ten minutes before we arrived. While it would have been nice, I didn't feel the need to be there with dad for his last breath, but I think my mom felt some regret.

That was the saddest day.

We always say, "It's a great day at Lapp Electric," but that was one day in the history of our company and our family that did not feel like a great day.

There's something my dad always said, and I have to admit that for a long time I didn't understand it.

"I owe everything to my parents," he'd say, and the more I found out about my Pop-Pop, the more I wondered. I could understand why my dad may have credited his mother with the way he turned out, but his father, too? I just didn't get it.

But you know, as I dug into my father's story, I realized that his parents, for the good and the bad, made him stronger. Everything in his life, every single thing that happened, made him more determined to live a certain way, to do certain things, and to avoid particular pitfalls.

That's what he meant, and that's why it's true.

We can all do that, you know. We can look at the things that happened to us in the past and use them to become better people, or we can use them as excuses as to why things didn't turn out the way we wanted.

You see it a lot, don't you? Parents fall short, and their children use that as an excuse for the rest of their lives. But it doesn't have to be that way. You can look at the most difficult circumstances of your life and say with pride, "That's why I became who I became. That's why I am who I am."

My brothers and I had the chance to say a few words at my father's memorial service. My brother Geoff had this to say:

I suspect that if you were here in person today you'd love on us with some powdered, crème-filled donuts, farmer's cheese, chocolate-covered almonds, warm Hammond's pretzels, or a couple of strombolis and pizzas along with, my personal favorite, Vanilla Coke to wash it down...

You certainly weren't immune to trouble and hardship (especially over the last five years), but you chose to live and love without complaint or argument. I want you to know that I noticed. I suspect that many of the people that are gathered here noticed too.

Being your son has been and always will be an honor and privilege to me. Recognizing your covenant to Mom for 43 years also was a testimony of your manhood to me. Dad, I know you wouldn't like me to brag on you in front of all these people, but I believe you uniquely had a way of loving me and those around you. It was grounded in a faith in God and manifested in your everyday living. Many of us reserve loving gestures or words for special events, but you made every occasion an opportunity to express love to others.

Geoff's words were moving and beautiful. My brother Greg echoed these sentiments in his own words:

Manny Lapp!! How can you even begin to describe him in words? He was a man who earned the respect of his peers in business by founding Lapp Electric and treating customers the way he would like to be treated. He was an entrepreneur, who created other opportunities by partnering with others who had strengths in other fields to help him be a better businessman. Those things are good, but what really defined dad was his love for his wife and family.

He would be amazed at all of the people who are here today because to him he was just living each day like it was a gift.

One of my dad's friends, Ron Martin, once said this of my dad. "I would do anything for Manny Lapp because I knew Manny Lapp would do anything for me."

That's how my dad was. He was generous with his time and resources. One of the things he would always say was that "People don't care how much you know until they know how much you care." He was a friend to everyone. He had relational equity with people because he always did what he said he was going to do. He always showed up.

We created a Lapper coin many years ago, and we give it to people who go above and beyond. Each letter stands for a trait that exemplifies my dad:

L – Leadership

A – Accessible

P – Positive Attitude

P – Perseverance

E – Enthusiastic

R – Reliable

That last one is the one that means the most to me personally. Being reliable. That was my dad, and that's who I strive to be, every single day.

Never blame others in your life for your misfortunes. Love even those who have hurt you. Keep moving forward.

Those are the takeaways I got from looking into the life of my father and his siblings.

You might be kicked out and rejected, but those who kept you going through all of it, your friends and family, those are the people who matter.

Learn from one generation to the next. Keep in mind the experiences of your parents and grandparents. Ask to hear their stories and think about how those stories are tangled in with your own story.

The negatives as well as the positives can guide you.

From shunning to shining.

My dad did it. I can do it.

So can you.

Begin Today
By Elam Stoltzfoos

So brief a time we have to stay,
Along this brief familiar way
It seems to me we should be kind,
To those whose lives touch yours and mine.

The hands that touch yours and mine,
Should we not help them when we may.
They are so kind that none can guess,
How soon they'll cease our hearts to bless.

The hands that love us soon may know,
How soon the long, long way must go.
Then might we not their faults forgive,
And make them happy while they live.

So many faults in life there are,
We need not go to seek them far.
But time is short and you and I,
Might let the little faults go by.

And ask for what is true and kind,
To those whose lives touch yours and mine.
These seem to me the better way,
Then why not friends, begin today.

Acknowledgments

I am especially thankful for my beautiful, patient, and sweet wife of 20 years. Marisa is God's greatest gift to me, and she continues to shine. I look forward with joy to spending my second half of life on this earth with her, God willing.

I often thought my life would be fulfilled if I got married and had a child. Well, God answered my prayers and blessed me with the gift of three wonderful children, Kali, Tegan, and Reese. Always remember you are God's best. I will always be your biggest fan.

I am truly grateful to Shawn Smucker for helping me compose this book. Without his expertise and excellence in writing, I would not have considered working on this book project during this season of my life.

I am also sincerely thankful to my mom, two brothers, plus my extended Lapp, Stull, Styer, and Wagner Family for your support and encouragement over the years. I love you all dearly and appreciate you more than you know.

Special thanks to my dad's friends and business associates that were always there for my dad...you know who you are, and there are too many to name individually. My dad always knew he could count on you to drive him for treatments at Johns Hopkins or just talk for hours about life and business. True and meaningful friendships are treasures.

Finally, to all of the employees (LAPPERs) past, present, and future at Lapp Electric. Thank you from the bottom of my heart! My father's shoes have been difficult ones to fill. Your patience and dedicated service throughout the last forty-six years is what made Lapp Electric great and truly a company that is "Powered By People."

The year 2015 marks the five-year anniversary of my dad's and pop pop's deaths, and it has been therapeutic for me to work on this story. As I am finishing up the writing of this book, my life long and dearest best friend chose to take his own life. It is in these times of darkness and deep personal tragedy where I need to continue to apply the principles and perseverance that my dad Manny Lapp taught me. His enduring legacy lives on in me, and I am forever grateful that he courageously lived a life of shunning to shining!

Godspeed,

Tim Lapp

Top Ten Most Memorable
Pop-Popisms:

As you probably picked up from the book, Pop-Pop was quite the character. Here are ten of his sayings that I'll never forget.

1. "Tell your troubles to Jesus." – I can't say Pop-Pop was the most sympathetic of men, and sometimes, if you told him something that sounded remotely like a complaint, he'd suggest you "tell your troubles to Jesus."
2. "1918…you do the math." – Sometimes I'd ask Pop-Pop how old he was. This was his standard reply.
3. "One boy's a boy, two boys are half a boy, and three boys are none."
4. "Don't talk so dumb."
5. "Whoop, whoop."
6. "Of course you know."
7. "Never kick your family off the farm." – I imagine this one came from personal experience.
8. "A father should never have to bury his child" – This is one I heard him say quite a few times after his son Wilmer's passing.
9. "If the sun shines on your ass, you're lazy."
10. "I'm going home." Amen, Pop-Pop. I look forward to seeing you all in heaven someday.

Tim Lapp has always been a family man, enjoying life with his wife and three children. He and his brothers also steward the family businesses their father and the Good Lord entrusted to them. Tim is Co-owner/CEO of Lapp Electrical Service, Inc. and Partner at East End Enterprises, LP. He received a bachelor's degree in Marketing from West Chester University. As an advocate for active engagement in community and leadership in business ethics, Tim has served on several non-profit boards and committees, and he has coached youth girls soccer and basketball.

Shawn Smucker has been co-writing since 2009 and has now authored or co-written nearly twenty books including the biography of Auntie Anne Beiler (*Twist of Faith*), the compelling story of a missionary dying of cancer (*Dying Out Loud*), and the moving story of a man whose son committed murder (*Refuse to Drown*). You can find him online at shawnsmucker.com. He lives in the city of Lancaster, PA, with his wife and five children.